1

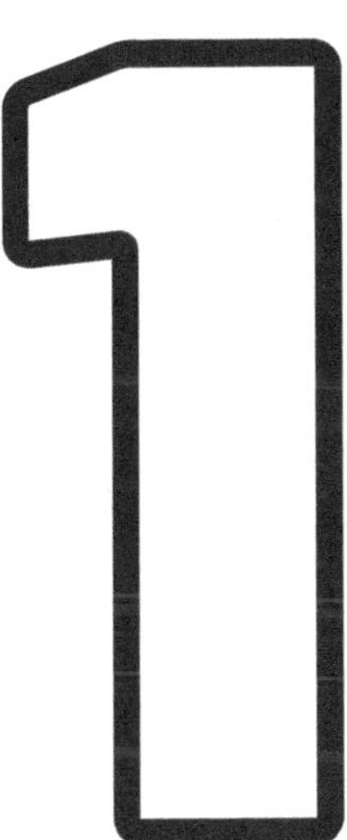

ONE

ONE

2

TWO

TWO

3

THREE

THREE

4

FOUR

FOUR

5

FIVE

FIVE

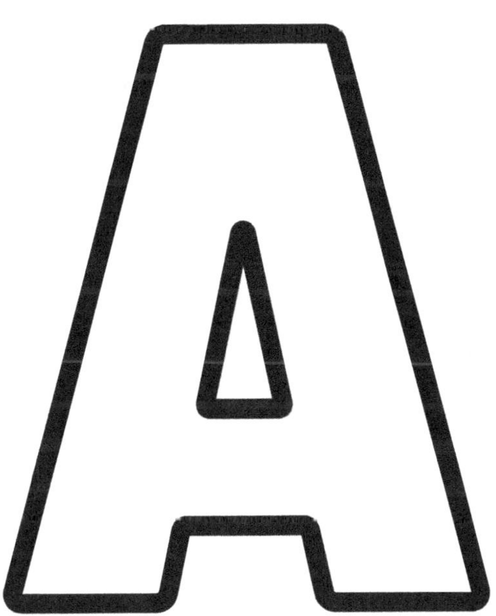

A

APPLE

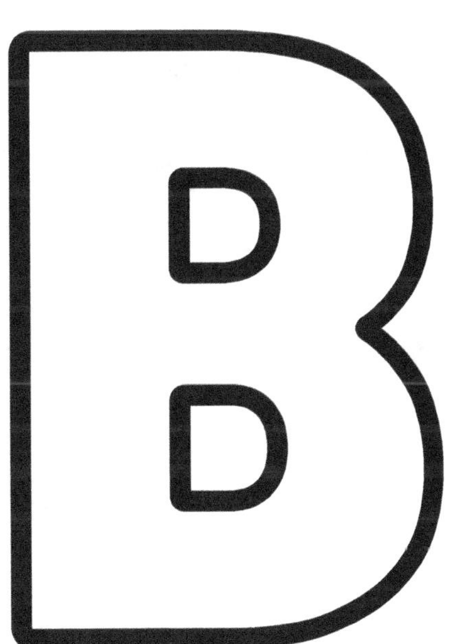

B

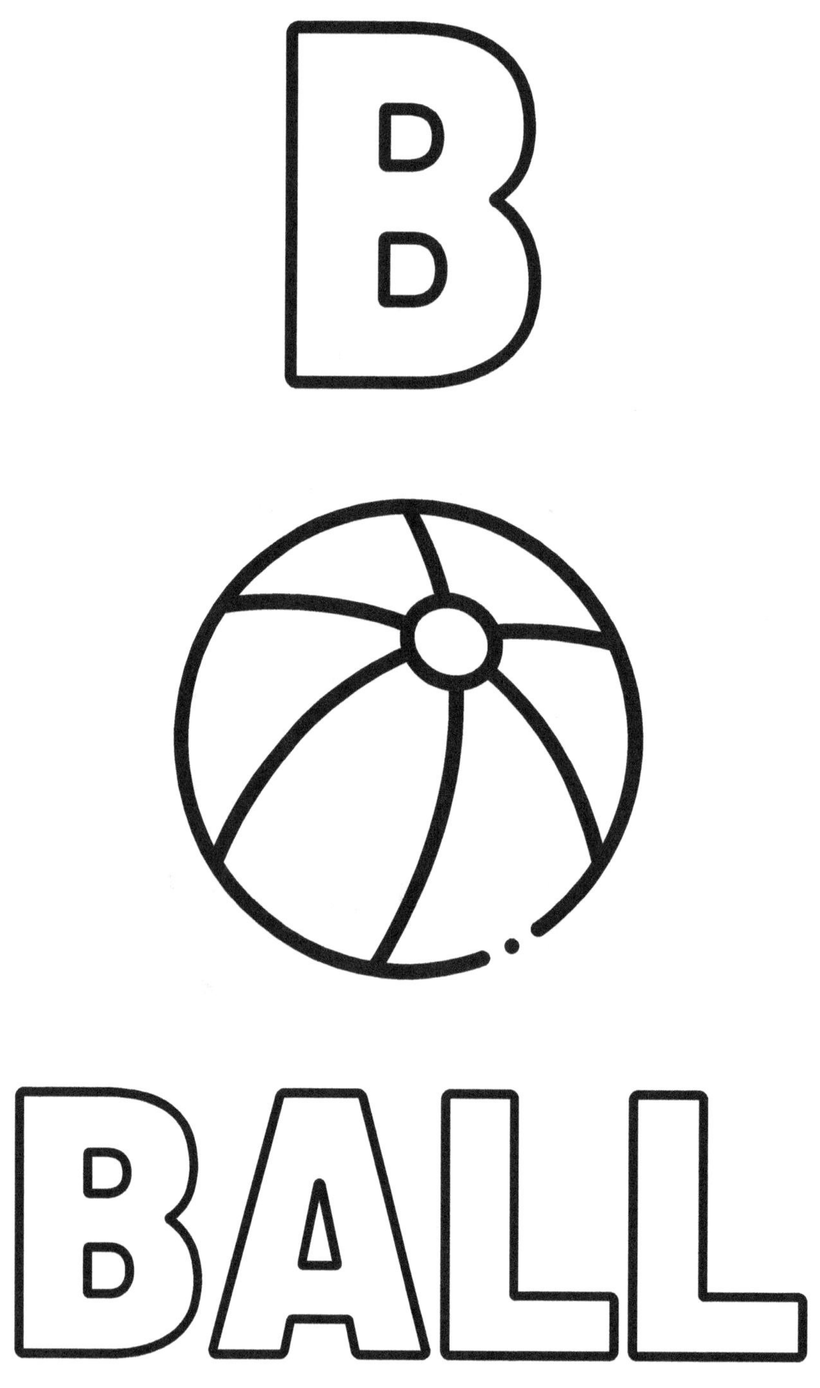

BALL

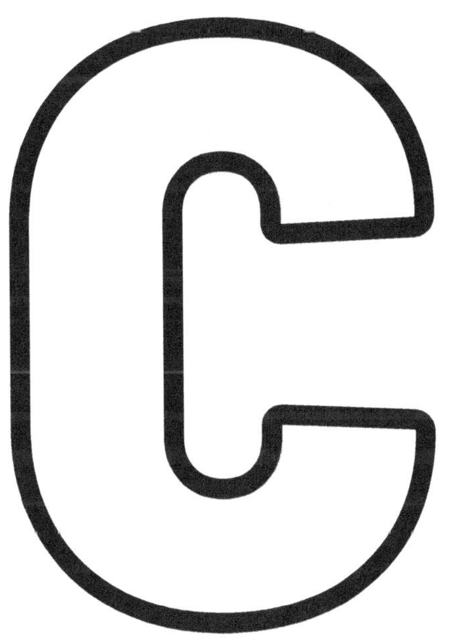

C

CAT

ABC

DEF

GHI

JKL

MNO

PQR

STU

VWX

YZ

123
456
789
10

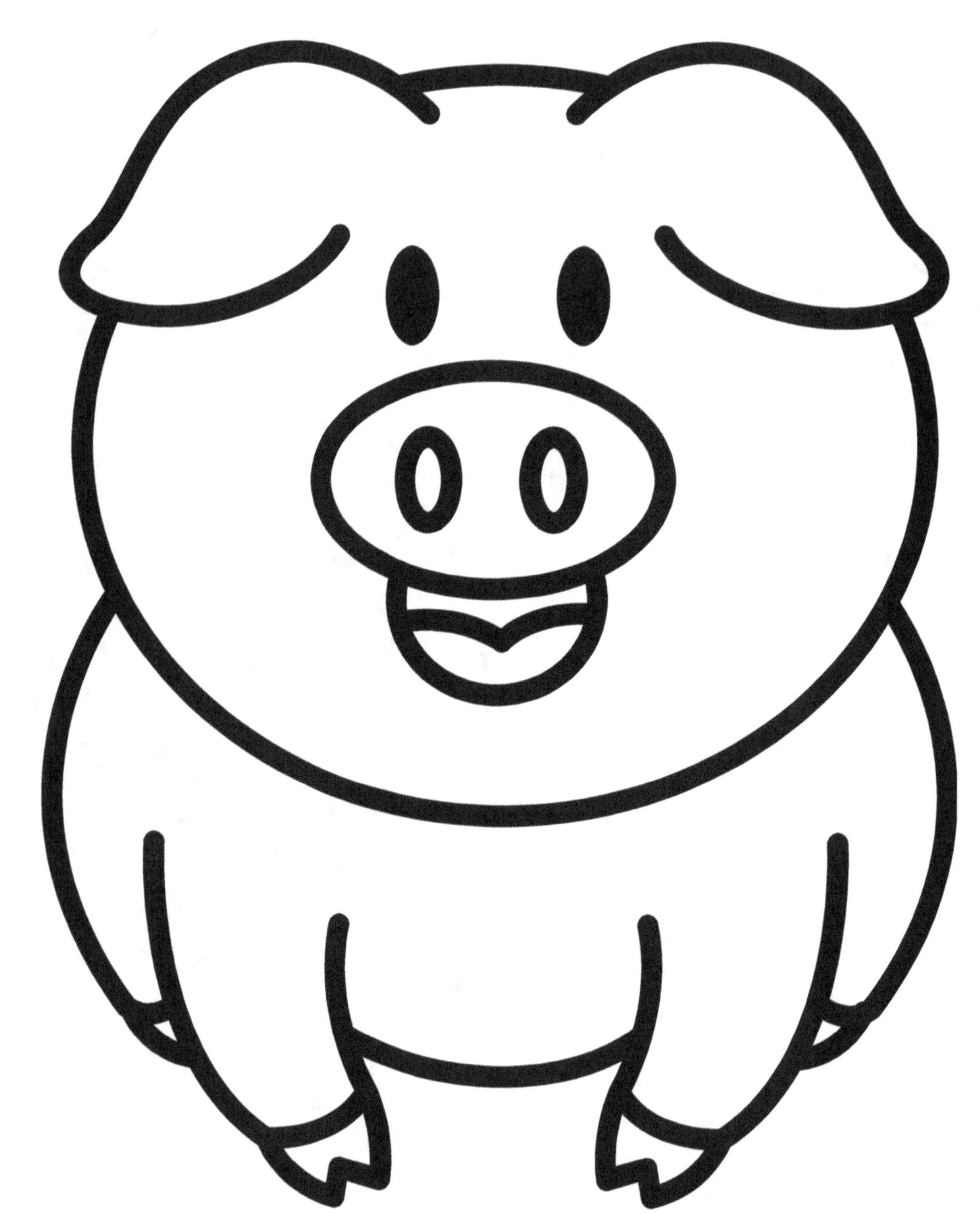

www.ingramcontent.com/pod-product-compliance
Lightning Source LLC
Chambersburg PA
CBHW080822120726
48001CB00009B/2969